To accomplish great things,
we must not only act,
but also dream,
not only plan,
but also believe.

— Anatole France

Keep Believing
in Yourself and Your Dreams

Words to Motivate and Inspire
Your Dreams

Edited by Patricia Wayant

Blue Mountain Press™
Boulder, Colorado

We wish to thank Susan Polis Schutz for permission to reprint the following poems that appear
in this publication: "Always Create Your Own Dreams and Live Life to the Fullest," "Live Your
World of Dreams," and "Do what you love…." Copyright © 1989, 1997, 2004 by Stephen Schutz
and Susan Polis Schutz. And for "It is so important…" and "This life is yours…." Copyright ©
1979 by Continental Publications. All rights reserved.

Library of Congress Control Number: 2007928378
ISBN: 978-1-59842-196-5

Acknowledgments appear on page 92.

▌▌ and Blue Mountain Press are registered in U.S. Patent and Trademark Office.
Certain trademarks are used under license.

Printed in China.
Fifth Printing: 2009

⊕ This book is printed on recycled paper.

This book is printed on archival quality, white felt, 110 lb. paper. This paper has been specially
produced to be acid free (neutral pH) and contains no groundwood or unbleached pulp. It
conforms with the requirements of the American National Standards Institute, Inc., so as
to ensure that this book will last and be enjoyed by future generations.

Blue Mountain Arts, Inc.
P.O. Box 4549, Boulder, Colorado 80306

Contents

Keep Believing in Yourself and Your Dreams

Every goal that has ever been reached began
   with just one step... and the belief that it
   could be attained.
Dreams really can come true, but they are
   most often the result of hard work,
   determination, and persistence.
When the end of the journey seems impossible
   to reach, all you need to do is take one
   more step.
Stay focused on your goal and remember that
   each small step will bring you a little closer.
When the road becomes hard to travel and it
   feels as if you'll never reach the end...
         Look deep inside your heart
         and you will find strength
         you never knew you had.

— Jason Blume

Focus on the Future...
and All You Might Be

Don't let old mistakes or misfortunes hold you down: learn from them, forgive yourself — or others — and move on. Do not be bothered or discouraged by adversity. Instead, meet it as a challenge. Be empowered by the courage it takes you to overcome obstacles. Learn something new every day.

Be interested in others and what they might teach you. But do not look for yourself in the faces of others. As far as who you are and who you will become goes — the answer is always within yourself. Follow your heart. You — like everyone else — will make mistakes. But as long as you are true to the strength within your own heart... you can never go wrong.

— Ashley Rice

Remember to Celebrate... YOU!

Celebrate all you are
and how much you are loved.
Honor the person you are
and all you're becoming.
Be reminded of how many people
look up to you and admire
all the goodness in your heart.
Reach out and feel the happiness
others wish for you.
Do the things
that bring sunlight to your heart
and add a touch of magic to your dreams.

— Linda E. Knight

Always Create Your Own Dreams and Live Life to the Fullest

Dreams can come true
if you take the time to
think about what you want in life...

Get to know yourself
Find out who you are
Choose your goals carefully
Be honest with yourself
Always believe in yourself
Find many interests and pursue them
Find out what is important to you
Find out what you are good at
Don't be afraid to make mistakes
Work hard to achieve successes
When things are not going right
don't give up — just try harder
Give yourself freedom to try out new things
Laugh and have a good time
Open yourself up to love
Take part in the beauty of nature
Be appreciative of all that you have
Help those less fortunate than you
Work toward peace in the world
Live life to the fullest
Create your own dreams and
follow them until they are a reality

— Susan Polis Schutz

On the Road to Your Dreams...

May you meet every challenge you are faced with, recognize every precious opportunity, and be blessed with the knowledge that you have the ability to make every day special.

May you be strong enough to keep your hopes alive. May you always be gentle enough to understand. May you know that you hold tomorrow within your hands and that the way there will be shared with the makings of what will be your most wonderful memories.

— R. L. Keith

...Don't Forget to Treasure the Journey

Remember all you have learned;
knowledge is the fuel for achievement.
Reflect on the lessons of life learned so far;
they add up to a priceless wisdom.
Appreciate the gift of choice available to you;
choose wisely and you will live well.
Listen to your inner voice;
it is the most important connection
    between your head and heart.
Leave self-doubt behind;
it serves only to make you hesitate.
Never stop questioning, searching,
    and reaching;
they are the only ways to stretch
    your mind and soul.
No matter what you do in this life,
remember it is never about
    the treasures you acquire;
it's about making certain
    it is *life* you treasure.

— Lisa Crofton

12/19/13

Don't wait for extraordinary opportunities. Seize common occasions and make them great.

— Orison Swett Marden

There Is No Limit to What You Can Achieve

Deep inside you
lies unlimited potential.
There are many ways
to tap into your talents,
but first you have to believe
in your power to create, to dream,
and to take risks.

The possibilities are unlimited
if you reach beyond what is comfortable.
Learn to accept change,
for it will help you realize
your inner strength and abilities.
To achieve your full potential,
learn to love without judgment,
create without inhibitions,
laugh without regrets,
and dream with no limitations.
Create your own destiny,
and success will follow you
on your journey.

— Jennifer Marsh

You Have What It Takes to Succeed

What you think of yourself is far more important than what others think of you.

There will be days when people will try to tear you down. Don't let them win. Hold your head high, walk proudly, and remember when you've done the best that you can do, there is nothing anyone can say to take that away from you.

Keep the song in your heart, and memorize it well. Play it over and over; soon others will take notice and look up to you. Some may even ask you for advice.

You have what it takes to succeed. You're a person of integrity, wisdom, and faith. If nagging doubts ever enter your mind, the kind where you question if what you're doing is right, pause for a moment, close your eyes, and just do what you need to do... believe.

— Kris Ackerman

Believe in the power of believing.
Say, "I believe," and believe it. Believe
in something, anything, that gives you
the courage and strength to continue
on when it would be so easy to give up.
Believe that you're beautiful. Believe it
when someone tells you, "You deserve
to be happy." Believe that you have
choices and that you can choose wisely.

— Rachel Snyder

Believe in what makes you feel good
and what makes you happy.
Believe in the dreams
you've always wanted to come true,
and give them every chance to.
If you are willing to take the
opportunities you are given
and utilize the abilities you have,
you will constantly fill
your life with special moments
and unforgettable times.
No one knows the mysteries of life
or its ultimate meaning,
but for those who are willing
to believe in their dreams
and in themselves,
life is a precious gift
in which anything is possible.

— Dena Dilaconi

Five Lessons to Live By as You Follow Your Dreams

Learn to laugh. Enjoy where you have been, where you are, and where you're going. Embrace the challenges you face along the way, and cherish the memories you make. Remember that what you see in life depends mainly on what you look for. Celebrate the simple joy of living, and open your heart to all life holds for you.

Learn to listen. Take time to slow down and be still, for sometimes it's only in silence you can hear your own heart. Listen to the wisdom it whispers and remain true to your destiny. Don't be afraid to admit when you are lost, because sometimes it's only by becoming lost that you can finally discover who you are and what you want from life. Don't be afraid to be yourself, and be brave enough to become the person you were meant to be.

Learn to let go. Allow your heart to heal from past hurts. Forgive failures and resolve regrets. Celebrate what was risked or attempted, improved or accomplished. and recognize that those who make no mistakes rarely make anything else, either.

Learn to love. Make commitments to what's important to you. Take risks for the things that truly matter. Remember love is not just something you feel, but the things you do. Give others the very best you have to offer, and leave the world a better place for what you have done and who you've been.

Learn to live. Don't be afraid of growing, changing, or living your life. No matter where you go or what you do, the true joy of life lies in the journey — not the destination. Search for your purpose, seek out your passions, and do what you love. It's not how long you live, but how you choose to live the days you are given, so choose to make the most of every opportunity you receive.

— Julie Anne Ford

Choose Your Dreams Wisely

12/10/13

It is so important
to choose your own
lifestyle
and not let others
choose it for you

— Susan Polis Schutz

Decisions are incredibly important things!
Good decisions will come back to bless you.
Bad decisions can come back to haunt you.

That's why it's so important that you take the
time to choose wisely.

Choose to do the things that will reflect
well... on your ability, your integrity, your
spirit, your health, your tomorrows, your
smiles, your dreams, and yourself.

There is someone who will thank you for
doing the things you do now with foresight
and wisdom and respect.

It's the person you will someday be.

You have a chance to make that person so
thankful and so proud. All you have to do is
remember these nine little words:

> Each time you come to a crossroads
> ...choose wisely.

— Douglas Pagels

Ten Important Traveling Companions to Take with You on the Journey to Your Dreams

1. Confidence: for when things get tough, when you're overwhelmed, when you think of giving up.

2. Patience: with your own trials and temptations, and with others.

3. An adjustable attitude: one that doesn't react, but responds with well-thought-out actions and feelings.

4. Beauty: within yourself, in your surroundings, and in nature.

5. Excitement: new things to enjoy and learn and experience.

6. Fun: laughter and smiles any way you can get them.

7. Companionship: people to share your happiness and sorrows, your troubles and joys.

8. Health: mental, physical, and emotional.

9. Peace: with others, yourself, and in your environment.

10. Love: pure, unconditional, and eternal.

— Barbara Cage

11/20/13

Do not wish to be anything
but what you are,
and try to be that perfectly.

— St. Francis de Sales

Boldly Be

Whatever is in you
to be,
whatever you love,
is your fire.
Ignite it, trust it;
it is a gift born of
your spirit.
Be it in words, dance,
colors, or a song...
have absolute faith
in what you
have been given;
chase it no matter
how elusive;
be it... however
challenging;
pursue it without pause;
seek to...
boldly be
whatever is in your
heart to be.

— Pam Reinke

Believe in Miracles!

Love your life.
Believe in your own power,
   your potential,
     and your innate goodness.
Every morning, wake with the awe
   of just being alive.
Each day, discover the magnificent,
   awesome beauty in the world.
Explore and embrace life in yourself
   and in everyone you see each day.
Reach within to find your own specialness.
Amaze yourself,
   and rouse those around you
     to the potential of each new day.

Don't be afraid to admit
    that you are less than perfect;
        this is the essence of your humanity.
Let those who love you help you.
Trust enough to be able to take.
Look with hope to the horizon of today,
    for today is all we truly have.
Live this day well.
Let a little sunshine out as well as in.
Create your own rainbows.
Be open to all your possibilities;
    possibilities can be miracles.
Always believe in miracles!

                    — Vickie M. Worsham

Life is not measured
by the number of
breaths we take,
but by the moments
that take our breath away.

— Author Unknown

Hold Fast Your Dreams

Hold fast your dreams!
Within your heart
Keep one still, secret spot
Where dreams may go,
And, sheltered so,
May thrive and grow
Where doubt and fear are not.
O keep a place apart,
Within your heart,
For little dreams to go!

We see so many ugly things —
Deceits and wrongs and quarrelings;
We know, alas! we know
How quickly fade
The color in the west,
The bloom upon the flower,
The bloom upon the breast,
And youth's blind hour.
Yet keep within your heart
A place apart
Where little dreams may go,
May thrive and grow.
Hold fast — hold fast your dreams!

— Louise Driscoll

Be a Dreamer Whose Dreams Come True

Dreams are images in your mind.
They're fantasies, goals, inventions,
hopes, visions, hearts' desires.
They can be fun to imagine,
they can keep you going,
and they can give you hope.
But they are still only dreams
until you make them real.

Dreamers whose dreams come true
    are realists.
They use self-control to actively
    pursue their dreams.
They take steps every day to make
    their dreams realities.
They forfeit some pleasures of today
for a life of greater value tomorrow.

Dreamers whose dreams come true
   are achievers.
They determine what it will take,
   and they resolve to do it.
They establish reasonable goals,
   and they meet them.
They set high expectations,
   and they strive for them.

Dreamers whose dreams come true
   are believers.
They see their dreams clearly.
They have faith that they can make
   them happen.
Their emotions, efforts, and actions
come from their desire and belief
that today's dreams are
   tomorrow's realities.

— Barbara Cage

Share Your Dreams with Others

12/19/13

Surround yourself with those who believe in you and who will help you achieve your goals.

— Lisa Marie Yost

Allow yourself to reach for the unattainable. Dream big. Act nobly. Attempt to master new things, knowing well that you may fail. It's okay to make mistakes as you stretch and grow. That is what makes us human, and that is how we become wiser. In reaching for our dreams, we often have to admit our vulnerability and ask for others' help. And the help is always close at hand. We are forever surrounded by teachers, from friends and family to a sage letter carrier, waitress, or carpool mom, who will share their life's wisdoms. Understand that seeking guidance and knowledge from your colleagues, elders, family, even acquaintances along the way, is the timeless mark of a truly wise person. We can only reach the summit, individually and collectively, if we are uplifted by one another.

— Susan Skog

Never Give Up Hope...

When the world says, "Give up,"
Hope whispers, "Try it one more time."

— Author Unknown

Optimism is the faith that
leads to achievement.
Nothing can be done
without hope or confidence.

— Helen Keller

Hope is such a marvelous thing.
It bends, it twists, it sometimes hides,
but rarely does it break.

Hope sustains us when nothing else can.
It gives us reason to continue
and the courage to move ahead
when we tell ourselves
we'd rather give in.

Hope puts smiles on our faces
when our hearts cannot manage.
Hope puts our feet on the path
when our eyes cannot see it.
Hope moves us to act when our souls
are confused by the direction.

Hope is a wonderful thing,
something to be cherished and nurtured,
and something that will
refresh us in return.
It can be found in each of us,
and it can bring light into
the darkest of places.

— Brenda Hager

In the Difficult Times, Keep Believing in Yourself

There are times in life
when things are not perfect,
when problems seem to surround you.

As you look for a way through
any problems that may occur,
it's important to keep
a positive attitude about your life
and where you are going.
You may wonder if you're making
the right choices.
You may wonder about how things
will turn out
if you take a different road.
But you are a strong
and motivated individual
who will rise to meet
the challenges that face you.
You will get through
the difficult times.

— Beverly A. Chisley

Know How to Overcome Failure

"Failure."
It's only a word.
But it carries with it so much pain
and so little concern,
so much frustration
and so little respect,
so much stress and so little
understanding
that people spend their lives
running through their days
in the hope of avoiding the long arm
of this little word.

To test your vision, you must risk
failure.

To temper your ego, you must attempt
the impossible.

To tell your story, you must
take a chance.

To see beyond the horizon, you must
　　　spread your wings.

To be all you can be, you must
　　stretch, flex, try, and go beyond
　　　your proven limits.

To bridge the silence, you must risk
　　rejection.

To advance into the unknown, you must
　　risk all your
　　　previous beliefs and emotions
　　that feel so secure.

Failure is not negative. It is a teacher.
It molds, refines, and polishes you
　　　so that one day your light will
　　　　shine for all to see.

It isn't the failure you experience
　　　that will determine your destiny,
　　but your next step and then the next
　　　that will tell
　　　　the story of your life.

— Tim Connor

Persevere and Carry On

It does not matter how slowly you go
so long as you do not stop.

— Confucius

Constant, slow movement
teaches us to keep working
like a small creek that stays clear,
that doesn't stagnate, but finds a way
through numerous details, deliberately.

— Rumi

People who fulfill their dreams are not merely lucky; neither are they necessarily the most talented. Rather, they understand the value of perseverance and determination. They believe that setbacks are simply a means to grow, and that small failures only pave the way for new insights. They know where they are going even when others do not and believe in their own dreams when others doubt. Their vision comes from within — and it is always burning in their hearts.

— Lisa Crofton

Your Hard Work Will Be Rewarded

12/18/13

The path to a dream is paved with sacrifices
and lined with determination.
And though it has many stumbling blocks
   along the way
and may go in more than one direction,
   it is traveled by belief and courage
and conquered with a willingness
   to face challenges and take chances.

— Barbara Cage

It is a rough road that leads to
the heights of greatness.

— Lucius Annaeus Seneca

Life Is Everything You Make It... and More

There will inevitably be obstacles to encounter. But don't worry that they will seem too great for you to handle, because you can. You may doubt yourself at times, but know that if you have faith, you have everything. Faith is the key to being successful.

If you know you are capable of anything because of who you are, you will always reach your destination. It may not always be easy, but it will always be worth it. Look ahead of you, never behind. Have faith in yourself. If you do, you will be amazed at what you can accomplish.

— T. L. Nash

Everything Will Fall
into Place

Life is like a giant puzzle.
Each of us has a picture in our minds
of how our lives will turn out...

We keep adding pieces to the puzzle,
     one at a time,
attempting to create that beautiful picture.
If one piece does not fit, we replace it
     with another.
We never get all the pieces in the right place
     on the first try.
It's all about experimenting until each piece
     fits together with the next.

Though our futures may not be clear
     or turn out exactly as we expected,
each of us has the strength inside to put
     the puzzle together.
We just have to look for the right pieces.
It may seem impossible, but keep striving.
Life's pieces have a way of falling into place
     when you least expect it.

— Renée M. Brtalik

Make Each Day Shine
One Day at a Time

You have a chance to be as happy
as any one person has ever been.
You have an opportunity to be as
proud as anyone you've ever known.
You have the potential to make a
very special dream come true.

And all you have to do...
is recognize the possibilities,
the power, and the wonder of... today.

It's right here, right now, and it
hopes and prays we will do the
right thing by recognizing it for the
golden opportunity... and the gift...
that it is.

Living life a day at a time means living a
life that is blessed with awareness,
appreciation, and accomplishment. For
one day, you can be everything you
were meant to be.

For one amazing day...

The weight is lifted. The path is clearer.
The goal is attainable. The prayer is
heard. The strength is sure. The courage
is complete. The belief is steady and
sweet and true.

For one remarkable day...

There is a brighter light in your life. The
will to walk up the mountain takes you
exactly where you want to go. The heart
understands what serenity really means.
And your hopes and wishes and dreams
will not disappear from view.

For one magnificent day...

You can live with an abundance of
love and goodness and grace
shining inside you.

— Douglas Pagels

What Is Success?

Success is in the way you walk
    the paths of life each day;
It's in the little things you do
    and in the things you say;
Success is in the glad hello
    you give your fellow man;
It's in the laughter of your home
    and all the joys you plan.

Success is not in getting rich
    or rising high to fame;
It's not alone in winning goals
    which all men hope to claim;
It's in the man you are each day,
    through happiness or care;
It's in the cheery words you speak
    and in the smile you wear.

Success is being big of heart
    and clean and broad of mind;
It's being faithful to your friends,
    and to the stranger, kind;
It's in the children whom you love,
    and all they learn from you —
Success depends on character
    and everything you do.

                — Edgar A. Guest

Remember What Is Most Important...

It's not having everything go right;
it's facing whatever goes wrong.
It's not being without fear;
it's having the determination
    to go on in spite of it.
It's not where you stand,
but the direction you're going in.
It's more than never having bad moments;
it's knowing you are always
    bigger than the moment.
It's believing you have already
    been given everything you need
        to handle life.

It's not being able to rid
   the world of all its injustices;
it's being able to rise above them.
It's the belief in your heart
   that there will always be
more good than bad in the world.

Remember to live just this one day
and not add tomorrow's troubles
   to today's load.
Remember that every day ends
and brings a new tomorrow
full of exciting new things.
Love what you do;
   do the best you can.

            — Vickie M. Worsham

Whatever you can do,
or dream you can... begin it.
Boldness has genius, power,
and magic in it.

— Johann Wolfgang von Goethe

You can do anything if
you have enthusiasm.

— Henry Ford

This life is yours
Take the power
to choose what you want to do
and do it well
Take the power
to love what you want in life
and love it honestly
Take the power
to walk in the forest
and be a part of nature
Take the power
to control your own life
No one else can do it for you
Take the power
to make your life
healthy
exciting
worthwhile
and very happy

— Susan Polis Schutz

See Yourself Succeeding

The way you see yourself
has a lasting impact on your life.
When you consider yourself
worthy of achieving your goals...
you'll become who you want to be.
You'll see yourself as confident and capable,
and you'll follow a different path —
because you now see yourself
    walking toward success.

We don't always realize
the full impact of our thoughts —
how far they reach
or how they truly affect us
    and our goals.
See yourself in this brand-new light.
Think you can — and you will.
Do all you can to become
everything you want to be.

— Barbara J. Hall

Let Your Spirit Shine Through!

You have an inner jewel. Let your spirit, the divine gem, shine through, and create a radiance about you wherever you go.

Let your mind be planted with seeds of love and joy and hope, and courage and universal goodwill and opulent harvest shall grow.

Think of each year as a sower scattering these seeds in your heart; then water them with the dews of sympathy, and throw open the windows to the broad sunlight of heaven while they ripen.

And — as surely as the days come and go — so surely shall your life grow.

— Ella Wheeler Wilcox

There's No Challenge
You Can't Face

Challenges make us stronger.
They push us to try harder.
They allow us to be brave.
They offer us courage.
They engender hope in us.
And sometimes we go farther
than we ever dreamed possible...
just by believing that we can.

— Ashley Rice

12/5/13

Believe
you are beautiful;
cherish your
uniqueness
and be
who you are;
through every hardship,
trust yourself
to overcome.
Be strong
when you can,
cry when you can't;
be wise
of the past
and embrace now!
Reach out
when you are safe,
hide when
you are not,
laugh often...
and listen carefully.
And never be afraid
to love yourself,
for that is where
all peace... is born.

— Pam Reinke

Go for It!

Have the daring to accept yourself
as a bundle of possibilities and
undertake the game of making the
most of your best.

— Henry Emerson Fosdick

What lies behind us
and what lies before us
are tiny matters
compared to what lies within us.

— Ralph Waldo Emerson

Let nothing hold you back from exploring
  your wildest fantasies, wishes, and
    aspirations.
Don't be afraid to follow your dreams
  wherever they lead you.
Open your eyes to their beauty;
open your mind to their magic;
open your heart to their possibilities.
Only by dreaming will you ever discover
who you are, what you want,
  and what you can do.
Don't be afraid to take risks,
  to become involved,
  to make a commitment.
Do whatever it takes to make
  your dreams come true.

— Julie Anne Ford

Dream the Impossible

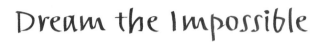

All who have accomplished
   great things
have had a great aim
and fixed their gaze
on a goal which was high —
one which sometimes seemed
   impossible.

— Orison Swett Marden

Some men see things
as they are and say, why?

I dream of things that
never were and say, why not?

— George Bernard Shaw

1/21/14 The future belongs to those who believe
in the beauty of their dreams.

— Marie Curie

1/28/14 Nothing is impossible to a willing heart.

— John Heywood

Visualize Your Dreams Coming True

You can use the creative power
of your mind
to confront and shape
your unique reality.
Believe that your vision is important;
this awareness will involve you
emotionally in your activities.
Develop the ability to love
and enjoy everything that you do;
see your projects and experiences
as an extension of yourself.
This total investment will account
for a large part of your success.

Let your imagination run rampant.
Once you have dreamed your final goal,
construct the mental pictures
of the steps you can take toward it.
Then go out with a heart
filled with passion
and actualize what you have seen.

This technique is called
"the power of visualization,"
and it has been proven effective
by many successful people.

When you have faith in the outcome,
no matter what it may be,
you cannot stop yourself
from living and working
with enthusiasm.
As you put what you feel into action,
you are filled with vitality and happiness.
When you start out
with an attitude like that,
it enriches your life
and mobilizes the people
around you.

When you act according to
your highest dreams,
the outcome is often
far grander than you might imagine.

— Wally Amos

Set Your Sights High

Dream lofty dreams,
and as you dream,
so shall you become.

— John Ruskin

They build too low who build
beneath the skies.

— Edward Young

Imagine... Here you are, on the high peak of a mountain. You can choose to wing your way toward the clouds, or you can simply walk the usual, ordinary paths that lead to the valley below.

Which choice will you make —
the well-worn paths or rising above it all?

>   Beautiful things await you
>   if you can reach the heights.

— George Sand

We can do whatever we wish to do provided our wish is strong enough.

— Katherine Mansfield

Be True to Yourself

Never let anyone change your mind about what you feel you can achieve.

Be true to the light that is deep within you. Hold on to your faith, hope, and joy for life. Keep good thoughts in your mind and good feelings in your heart. Keep love in your life, and you will find the love and light in everyone.

Be giving, forgiving, patient, and kind. Have faith in yourself. Be your own best friend, and listen to the voice that tells you to be your best self.

Be true to yourself in the paths that you choose. Follow your talents and passions; don't take the roads others say you must follow because they are the most popular. Take the paths where your talents will thrive — the ones that will keep your spirits alive with enthusiasm and everlasting joy.

Most of all, never forget that there is no brighter light than the one within you. Follow your inner light to your own personal greatness.

— Jacqueline Schiff

Be what you are,
and become
what you are capable
of becoming.

— Robert Louis Stevenson

1/23/14

Do what you love
Control your own life
Have imaginative
    realistic dreams
Work hard
Make mistakes
    but learn from them
Believe in yourself but
    know your limitations
Ignore people who tell you
    that you can't
Plow through obstacles
    and failures
Try to turn your dreams
    into reality

— Susan Pols Schutz

Make Your Life
the Best It Can Be

Each new day is a blank page in the diary
of your life. The pen is in your hand, but
the lines will not all be written the way you
choose; some will come from the world
and the circumstances that surround you.
But for the many things that *are* in your
control, remember this...

The secret of life is in making your story as
beautiful as it can be. Write the diary of your
days and fill the pages with words that come
from the heart. As the pages take you
through time, you will discover paths that
will add to your happiness and your
sorrows, but if you can do these things,
there will always be hope in your tomorrows.

Follow your dreams. Work hard. Be kind. This is all anyone could ever ask: do what you can to make the door open on a day that is filled with beauty in some special way. Remember: goodness will be rewarded. Smiles will pay you back. Have fun. Find strength. Be truthful. Have faith. Don't focus on the things you lack.

Realize that people are the treasures in life and happiness is the real wealth. Have a diary that describes how you are doing your best, and...

The rest will take care of itself.

— Douglas Pagels

Don't Let Anything Stand in the Way of Your Dreams

Catch the star that holds your destiny —
the one that forever twinkles
within your heart
Take advantage of precious opportunities
while they still sparkle before you
Always believe that your ultimate goal
is attainable as long as you
commit yourself to it

Though barriers may sometimes
stand in the way of your dreams
remember that your destiny is hiding behind them
Accept the fact that not everyone
is going to approve of the choices you make
but have faith in your judgment
Catch the star that twinkles in your heart
and it will lead you to your destiny's path
Follow that pathway and uncover the
sweet sunrises that await you
Take pride in your accomplishments
as they are steppingstones to your dreams
Understand that you may make mistakes
but don't let them discourage you
Value your capabilities and talents
for they are what make you truly unique
The greatest gifts in life are not purchased
but acquired through hard work
and determination
Find the star that twinkles in your heart
for you are capable of making
your brightest dreams come true
Give your hopes everything you've got
and you will catch the star
that holds your destiny

— Shannon M. Lester

He who is bound to a star
does not turn back.

— Leonardo da Vinci

Dreams are like stars — you may never
touch them, but if you follow them they
will lead you to your destiny.

— Author Unknown

Ah, great it is to believe the dream
As we stand in youth by the starry stream;
But a greater thing is to fight life through,
And say at the end, "The dream is true!"

— Edwin Markham

Just for today...
wish on a star
It doesn't matter
how far away it seems.
Follow your bliss.
Greet the dawn
with a smile.

Just for today...
touch a moonbeam.
Let your inner light shine.
Discover all the potential
inside you.
Do the things that
make your heart happy.
Remember your hopes
are closer than you think.

Just for today...
start fresh; begin anew.
Leave regrets behind.
A whole new world is
ahead of you.
Count your blessings
and realize you're loved
more than you know —
today and every tomorrow.

— Linda E. Knight

All You Have to Do...
Is Believe

12/29/13

To accomplish great things,
we must not only act,
but also dream,
not only plan,
but also believe.

— Anatole France

Once you believe —
big things can happen in your life,
because believing
makes all the difference
in achieving your dreams.
Once you begin
to see yourself succeeding — you will.
Once you imagine a happy ending —
    you'll work for one.
Your way of thinking is the key;
it starts from there
and will progress the way
you want it to.
Once you believe —
you're on your way.
Your wildest dreams can't compare
to what will happen next.
You're the creator and planner
    of your own destiny;
you're the only one who can make
big things happen in your life.
Start believing... and make it all
    come true.

— Barbara J. Hall

Your Dreams May Be Closer Than You Think

You are driven to reach dreams that will make your future so much brighter. You have an inner spark that kindles a light in everyone your life touches.

Keep on flying with your highest dreams, and believe they will carry you where you want to go. Say "yes" to challenges, and dare to make those big, bold dreams come true.

Tend the fires of your passions and use this energy to do good in life. Keep your deepest passions alive and active. Fly on the wings of your talents and your mightiest dreams.

— Jacqueline Schiff

If you believe you can, you will.
Stay focused on what you want to happen,
and don't lose sight of the goals ahead.
You are never alone when you
    have others who believe in you.
Borrow their faith in you if yours
    is running low.
When you think you can't take
    another step,
someone will help you find a way,
even if they must carry you for a while.
And always remember...
only by believing in your dreams
will you ever know what you are
    capable of achieving.
Only by believing in yourself
will your dreams come true.
So reach down deep inside,
    bring them out,
        and make them come to life.

— Elizabeth Ann Nichols

Don't Ever Stop Dreaming Your Dreams

Don't ever try to understand everything —
some things will just never make sense.
Don't ever be reluctant to show your feelings:
When you're happy, give in to it!
When you're not, live with it.

Don't ever be afraid to try to
   make things better —
   you might be surprised at the results.
Don't ever take the weight of the world
   on your shoulders.
Don't ever feel threatened by the future —
   take life one day at a time.
Don't ever feel guilty about the past —
   what's done is done. Learn from any
   mistakes you might have made.
Don't ever feel that you are alone —
   there is always somebody there for you
   to reach out to.
Don't ever forget that you can achieve
   so many of the things you can imagine —
   imagine that! It's not as hard as it seems.
Don't ever stop loving,
   don't ever stop believing,
      don't ever stop dreaming your dreams.

— Laine Parsons

Refuse to Let Anything Steal Your Joy

Choose to be well in every way. Choose to be happy no matter what. Decide that each day will be good just because you're alive.

You have power over your thoughts and feelings. Don't let your circumstances dictate how you feel. Don't let your thoughts and feelings color your situation blue or desperate.

Even if you don't have everything you want, even if you're in pain or in need, you can choose to be joyful no matter what you're experiencing. You are more than your body, your physical presence, and your material possessions. You are spirit. You have your mind, heart, and soul, and there is always something to be thankful for.

Decide that life is good and you are special. Decide to enjoy today. Decide that you will live life to the fullest now, no matter what. Trust that you will change what needs changing, but also decide that you're not going to put off enjoying life just because you don't have everything you want now. Steadfastly refuse to let anything steal your joy. Choose to be happy... and you will be!

— Donna Fargo

Let your dreams take you...
to the corners of your smiles,
to the highest of your hopes,
to the windows of your
opportunities,
and to the
most special places
your heart
has ever known.

— Carson Wrenn

Live Your World of Dreams

Lean against a tree
and dream your world of dreams
Work hard at what you like to do
and try to overcome all obstacles
Laugh at your mistakes
and praise yourself for learning from them
Pick some flowers
and appreciate the beauty of nature
Be honest with people
and enjoy the good in them
Don't be afraid to show your emotions
Laughing and crying make you feel better
Love your friends and family
    with your entire being
They are the most important part of your life
Feel the calmness on a quiet sunny day
and plan what you want to accomplish in life
Find a rainbow
and live your
world of dreams

— Susan Polis Schutz

You Have Everything You Need to Take You Where You Want to Go

You have abilities and talents and attributes
that belong to you alone, and you have
what it takes to make your path of success...
lead to happiness.

You have qualities that get better every day!
You have the courage and strength to see
things through.
You have smiles that will serve as your guides.
You have a light that will shine in you 'til the
end of time.

You have known the truth of yesterday, and
you have an inner map that will lead the
way to a very beautiful tomorrow.
You have gifts that have never even been
opened and personal journeys waiting to be
explored. You have *so much* going for you.
You are a special person, and you have a
future that is in the best of hands. And you
need to remember: if you have plans you
want to act on and dreams you've always
wanted to come true...

You have what it takes, because...
You have you.

— Douglas Pagels

May All Your Dreams Come True

May you know, in your heart, that
others are always thinking of you.
May you always have rainbows that
follow the rain.
May you celebrate the wonderful things
about you.
And when tomorrow comes, may you
do it all over again.

May you remember how full of smiles
    the days can be.
May you believe that what you search for,
    you will see.
May you find time to smell the flowers
    and to share the beauty of you.
May you envision today as a gift
    and tomorrow as another.
May you add a meaningful page to the
    diary of each new day,
    and may you make
    "living happily ever after..."
    something that will really come true.

And may you always keep planting
    the seeds of your dreams.
      Because if you keep
        believing in them,
    they'll keep trying their best...
      to blossom for you.

                — Collin McCarty

ACKNOWLEDGMENTS

We gratefully acknowledge the permission granted by the following authors and authors' representatives to reprint poems or excerpts from their publications.

Jason Blume for "Keep Believing in Yourself and Your Dreams." Copyright © 2005 by Jason Blume. All rights reserved.

Lisa Crofton for "On the Road to Your Dreams..." and "People who fulfill their dreams...." Copyright © 2007 by Lisa Crofton. All rights reserved.

Jennifer Marsh for "There Is No Limit to What You Can Achieve." Copyright © 2007 by Jennifer Marsh. All rights reserved.

Kris Ackerman for "You Have What It Takes to Succeed." Copyright © 2007 by Kris Ackerman. All rights reserved.

Rachel Snyder for "Believe...." Copyright © 2007 by Rachel Snyder. All rights reserved.

Julie Anne Ford for "Five Lessons to Live By as You Follow Your Dreams." Copyright © 2007 by Julie Anne Ford. All rights reserved.

Pam Reinke for "Boldly Be" and "Believe you are beautiful...." Copyright © 2007 by Pam Reinke. All rights reserved.

Barbara Cage for "Be a Dreamer Whose Dreams Come True." Copyright © 2007 by Barbara Cage. All rights reserved.

Susan Skog for "Allow yourself to reach for...." Copyright © 2007 by Susan Skog. All rights reserved.

Brenda Hager for "Hope is such a marvelous thing." Copyright © 2007 by Brenda Hager. All rights reserved.

Tim Connor for "Know How to Overcome Failure." Copyright © 2005 by Tim Connor. All rights reserved.

Barbara J. Hall for "See Yourself Succeeding" and "Once you believe...." Copyright © 2007 by Barbara J. Hall. All rights reserved.

Wally Amos for "Visualize Your Dreams Come True." Copyright © 2006 by Wally Amos. All rights reserved.

Linda E. Knight for "Just for today...." Copyright © 2007 by Linda E. Knight. All rights reserved.

Elizabeth Ann Nichols for "If you believe you can, you will." Copyright © by Elizabeth Ann Nichols. All rights reserved.

PrimaDonna Entertainment Corp. for "Refuse to Let Anything Steal Your Joy" by Donna Fargo. Copyright © 2006 by PrimaDonna Entertainment Corp. All rights reserved.

A careful effort has been made to trace the ownership of selections used in this anthology in order to obtain permission to reprint copyrighted material and give proper credit to the copyright owners. If any error or omission has occurred, it is completely inadvertent, and we would like to make corrections in future editions provided that written notification is made to the publisher:

BLUE MOUNTAIN ARTS, INC., P.O. Box 4549, Boulder, Colorado 80306.